Mochi-Celeste
GOES TO
WASHINGTON D.C.

Written and Illustrated by Edgar & Yuriko Justus

On Board

ARE WE
THERE YET?

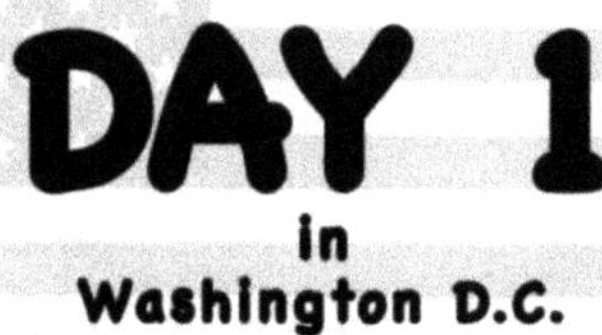

DAY 1
in
Washington D.C.

I've seen
BETTER

DAY 2

in

Washington D.C.

SO NOT
IMPRESSED
U.S. Constitution
We the People

DAY 3

in
Washington D.C.

Not High
ENOUGH

DAY 4

in
Washington D.C.

I found my

NEW BED

DAY 5

in
Washington D.C.

Found a
CONGRESS OF THE UNITED STATES
SHADY SPOT

Later
That Day

I can do better
U. S. CONGRESS
THAN YOU

DAY 6

Runs for Office

Mochi-Celeste for PRESIDENT
Universal Health Care
(Hoomans Not Applicable)
0% Unemployment Rate
(24/7 Catnip Production)
Honest Tax Reform
(All Proceeds Go To Me)
Government Transparency
(My Needs Come First)
"You Exist To FEED ME"

Presidential Debate

I HATE YOU 
Mochi-Celeste FIRST
Presidential Race
VOTE FOR ME

Election Day

I'm NOT

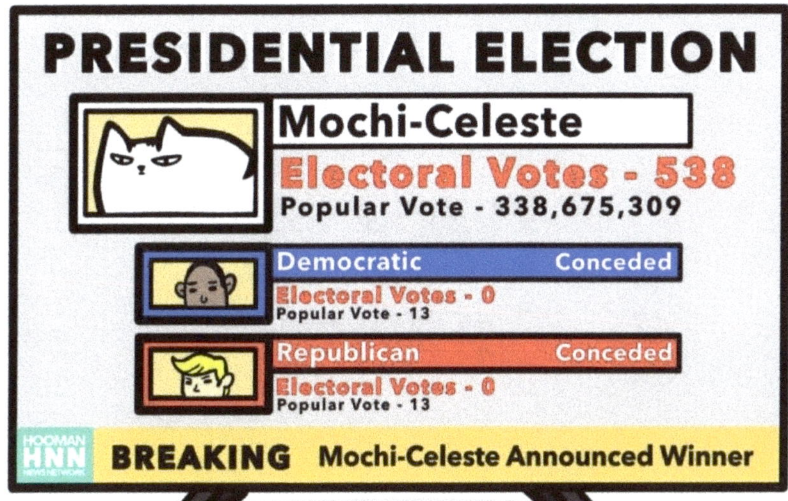

EVEN TRYING

DAY 1

AS PRESIDENT
(Oath of Office)

I am
THE BOSS
PRESIDENT OF THE UNITED STATES
SEAL OF THE PRESIDENT OF THE UNITED STATES
E UNITED STAT

DAY 2
AS PRESIDENT

BOSS

This is BORING

A Few
Moments Later

BOSS

DAY 3
AS PRESIDENT

MADE
IT
BETTER

DAY 4
AS PRESIDENT

NOT GOOD ENOUGH

A Few
Moments Later

DAY 5

AS PRESIDENT

Built it
BETTER

DAY 6
AS PRESIDENT

NEVER SATISFIED

A Few
Moments Later

OFFSHORE BANK TO TOP
HOW TO LIE
How to Issue Exec Orders
HOO-MAN TRAI-NING
DOSS

A Few Moments
Later After
That...

DAY 7

(Mochi-Celeste Independence Day)

AREA51
Made in China
BOOM
BEST PRESIDENT EVER

DAY 8

AS PRESIDENT
(Impeached)

I'm ABOVE THE LAW

DAY 9

AS PRESIDENT
(Stands Trial)

GO FASTER
DEPARTMENT OF CORRECTIONS

DAY 10

LAST DAY AS PRESIDENT
(Removed from Office)

I'm plotting

YOUR DEMISE

YOU ARE
DOOMED

Mochi-Celeste Empire LLC
PO Box 528. Hanapepe, Hawaii 96716
www.mochiceleste.com

24 25 26 27 28 WHO 6 5 4 3 2 1
First Edition, 2024
Second Edition (Resized; Revised), 2024

Library of Meowness Catalog-in-Publication Data
Justus, Edgar; Kihara, Yuriko; Justus, Yuriko,
Mochi-Celeste. Washington DC. Humor.]
Mochi-Celeste : Washington D.C., 2024/ Edgar Justus and Yuriko Kihara (Yuriko Justus)
Collection of humorous sayings collected with drawings of Mochi-Celeste in Washington, DC,
based on the late Celeste_the_Cat_Boss of Instagram, located at Talk Story Bookstore in Hawaii.
ISBN: 979-8-2184-0128-3
1. Mochi-Celeste.   2. Humor.   3. Justus, Edgar.   4. Kihara, Yuriko.   4a. Justus, Yuriko.   5. Cats.
6. United States.   7. Washington DC.   8. Elections.   9. Presidents.   10. Imprisonment.   I. Title.

PN7734.C03W8088675309
170.1'015-dc51
8218378721

Design: Edgar Justus and Yuriko Kihara (Yuriko Justus)

9 798218 401283